MW01165178

Working Together Against

WORLD
HUNGER

Hunger is a devastating tragedy all over the world.

❖THE LIBRARY OF SOCIAL ACTIVISM❖

Working Together Against

WORLD HUNGER

Nancy Bohac Flood

THE ROSEN PUBLISHING GROUP, INC.
NEW YORK

Published in 1995 by The Rosen Publishing Group, Inc.
29 East 21st Street, New York, NY 10010

First Edition

Library of Congress Cataloging-in-Publication Data

Flood, Nancy Bohac.
    Working together against world hunger / Nancy Bohac Flood. — 1st
ed.
        p.   cm. — (The Library of social activism)
    Includes bibliographical references and index.
    ISBN 0-8239-1773-8
    1. Food relief—Juvenile literature.   2. Social action—Juvenile
literature.   [1. Food relief.   2. Hunger.   3. Social action.]
    I. Title.   II. Series.
    HV696.F6F578 1995
    363.8—dc20   95-6858
                                                                            CIP
                                                                            AC

Manufactured in the United States of America

20628

Contents

1. Every Day—Forty Thousand Children   7

2. Hunger—The World's Silent Catastrophe   11

3. A Million Candles Burning   26

4. How You Can Help   33

5. More Choices: Working Against Hunger   41

6. Make a Difference   48

7. "If People Weren't Eating, What Else Mattered?" Frances Moore Lappé   52

8. What Have We Done? Where Are We Going?   56

Glossary   59

Organizations to Contact   60

Further Reading   62

Index   63

Death squads have been hired by local merchants to kill some of the hundreds of homeless children in Rio de Janeiro.

chapter

1

EVERY DAY—FORTY THOUSAND CHILDREN

THIS BOOK IS NOT MEANT TO UPSET YOU OR make you feel depressed or guilty that you have a good home and plenty to eat. But it is meant to make you aware, and to start you thinking of your own life in relation to all life on our planet. There are many ways that you can help make a better world, and this book will help you see how your actions can help make a difference.

Rio de Janeiro—Friday morning July 23, 1993. In the predawn shadows of Candelaria Cathedral, two police officers began shooting. When they finished, seven children lay dead. They had been sleeping with forty others on cardboard scraps.

These children ranging in age from eight to fifteen, were a few of the seven million children who live on Rio's city streets without homes and often without food. Each day children are gunned down by police and other death squads, paid for by merchants.

One out of five children in the United States grows up hungry.

Imagine that you are watching this newscast in your sociology class. The picture before you now fades as one of the street boys kicks at a cardboard square that had been his bed. He slips into the crowd of people, eyes downcast but searching, always searching, for ways to find food—and survive.

Another picture fills the screen: a city playground.

Swings squeak back and forth. One child sits in the dirt watching while four children run to the swings. They give the seats a big push, jump on, and then swoop high, laughing while pumping their legs, pushing themselves higher.

One child watches and four children play. In most industrialized countries, one child out of five is too hungry to play.

This scene is not in a poor or war-torn country. This scene is in the United States. One child out of every five in the United States grows up hungry—and angry—as a result of abuse, indifference, and hunger.

In poorer countries, one out of three children die from starvation before their fifth birthday.

Every day forty thousand children die because they don't have enough to eat.

Imagine you are back in your home-room. The students begin talking, asking questions, and arguing:

"If so many kids are starving, why doesn't someone send them food?"

"Forty thousand kids dead every day! Is there even enough food to feed them?"

"But maybe there is enough food. Doesn't anyone care?"

"Good question. Isn't anyone doing anything? What could we do?"

"Send them food, stupid."

"Not just food. That helps in an emergency, like a famine or an earthquake. You know, like Somalia or India."

"People needed food after that hurricane leveled Florida."

"Yeah, and the Mississippi flooded out whole cities."

"People also needed clothes and houses."

"And books. Remember? Our school collected books."

"But then we couldn't send the books until the homes and schools were rebuilt. What good is a book if you don't have a house?"

"What good is anything if you don't have food?"

"How about the street kids being killed in Rio? Can't the U.N. or the Red Cross or someone stop it?"

"I don't know. I keep thinking about those starving people, especially the little children. Kids like me being shot just because they're hungry and homeless. There must be something we can do."

❖ QUESTIONS TO ASK YOURSELF ❖

Children are dying from the effects of poverty and hunger all over the world. Let's think about how this might affect you. 1) Why is world hunger an important issue to you? 2) The media has made the public aware of starvation in Somalia. What other countries are faced with the devastation of hunger? 3) Is the United States one of those countries?

chapter

2

HUNGER—THE WORLD'S SILENT CATASTROPHE

EIGHTY-SIX MILLION PEOPLE IN BRAZIL DO not have enough to eat.

For seven million children, obtaining food means begging or stealing. Bed means a piece of cardboard. School . . . impossible and meaningless. Finding food is all that counts. Without education or job skills, the future for these children is homelessness, hunger, and early death.

Brazil is only one country of many where children don't have enough to eat. How much hunger is in our world?

You can see on the map on pages 12 and 13 that many countries are shaded gray. The gray indicates hunger. Hunger affects the whole world.

❖ WHAT DOES IT MEAN TO BE ❖ HUNGRY ALL THE TIME?

Eloy Casorla was 16 when police killed his father for organizing workers in the tin mines of

Bolivia. Eloy's mother could not earn enough to feed the family. Eloy knew what he must do.

The streets of Cochabamba became his home. Hustling became his life—washing cars, shining shoes, and stealing. He did anything—so he could send money back home.

Where Do the Hungry People Live?
Countries with an infant mortality rate of 50 per 1000 or above are shaded.

Imagine Eloy's life. Imagine his home.

It's dark. No electricity, which means there's nothing that requires electricity. No TV, radio, refrigerator, or CD. A phone? Forget it—there isn't even running water.

Inside there's one wooden bench. No couch

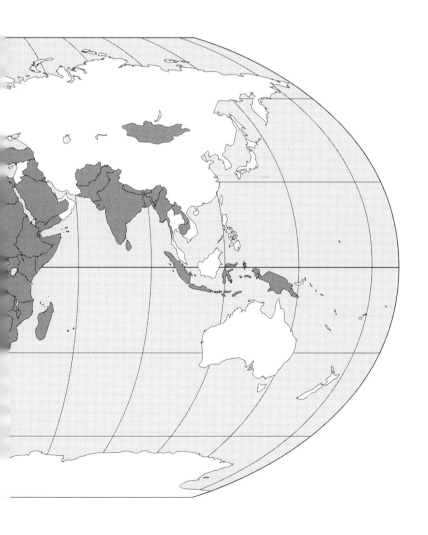

or beds. No books or magazines. A closet? No, but no one has extra clothes or extra anything.

There's almost nothing to eat. Nothing in the cupboard except a bag of rice, some beans, salt and matches.

Eloy's mother, brothers and sisters live in this one-room house. His uncle and his family live here too so they can help pay the rent. The road outside is dirt. Trees? A tree means wood for cooking a meal. Flowers? None. Mail? The house has no address. A school? His younger brothers could go if they walked to it. It's a few miles away. They don't have the required uniform, shoes, pencils, paper, or a light to study by. They are too busy harvesting coffee beans for sixty-five cents a day. They will stay poor and hungry. They won't live long—unless . . .

Two out of every ten people are hurt by hunger. One child out of every three does not grow properly because of not having enough to eat. These children have enough to stay alive for a few years, but their bodies become weak. Eventually they die from starvation.

❖ JUST WHAT IS CHRONIC HUNGER? ❖

Chronic hunger means being hungry all the time and not having enough food for the brain and body to grow properly. Minimum food means staying alive but not growing strong. One measurement of chronic hunger is the infant death rate.

For some, begging is the only way to survive.

In the nations tinted gray on the map, fifty out of every thousand children die before their first birthday.

For each of thirty people in these countries the following statistics apply:

dying before age 50 . . . . . 9 out of 30
being undernourished . . . 10 out of 30
earning less than $600 . . 17 out of 30
    a year
never learning to read . . . 21 out of 30

15

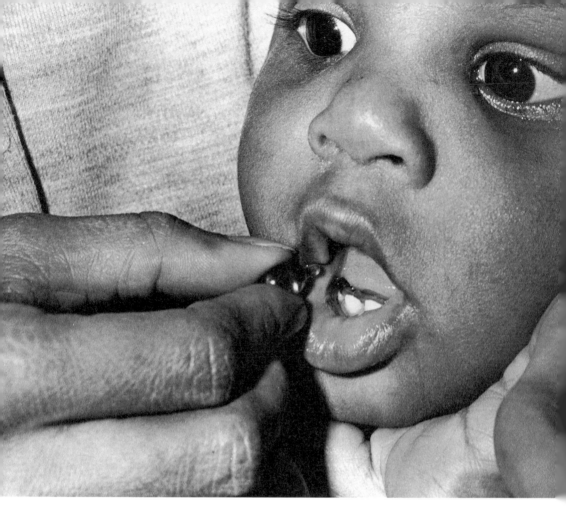

A worker from the Helen Keller Institute administers a large dose of Vitamin A to help save this child's sight from the effects of malnutrition.

never attending school . . 6 out of 30
drinking polluted water . . 15 out of 30

Chronic hunger kills slowly over time. Every year hunger kills more people than any war or disaster.

❖ **HOW DOES HUNGER KILL?** ❖

Chronic hunger is not the cause of death but it begins the process.

Chronic hunger increases the damage from other diseases. A malnourished child gets sick easily because the immune system and internal organs such as the heart have been weakened.

Chronic hunger causes blindness. Xerophthalmia is an eye disease resulting from poor nutrition, specifically, lack of Vitamin A.

Ramona's family didn't have money to buy vegetables. Mostly they ate rice and sometimes, nothing. Ramona's stomach hurt. Sometimes her head and eyes hurt too. It was hard to walk all the way to school with nothing in her stomach. It was too hard to read her school books. More and more the world looked dark. The sun was dim, not bright.

Two pills of Vitamin A a year, costing about ten cents, can save one child's sight. Helen Keller International and International Eye Foundation sponsor programs to fight blindness worldwide. Their addresses are listed in the appendix.

Hunger damages the body and the brain. Malnutrition during pregnancy is destructive to the growing fetus. Children can be born with brain damage, which is often permanent.

A starving brain cannot work properly. A starving person becomes confused, unaware and uncaring.

Hunger harms the human spirit. In his book, *Living Poor*, Moritz Thomsen, an American,

writes about his Peace Corps experience in
Ecuador. During a drought people "were selling
their children before they died of hunger; autop-
sies on the ones who had died revealed stomachs
full of roots and dirt."

"This year the money made from my crop
of coffee, I will use to pay my mortgage.
For one more year my farm cannot be
taken from me. But if my child gets sick, I
will have no money to pay for a bus to
take me to the clinic for treatment and
medicine. But without (my farm) my child
will die anyway. With no farm, I have no
money, no food. But today my youngest
died, from fever and diarrhea. Take my
farm. Take it; I don't care."

adapted from *Witness to War*,
written by Dr. Charles Clements, an
Air Force pilot and Vietnam veteran,
about his experiences in El Salvador.

Why is there hunger?

❖ **IS THERE ENOUGH FOOD? YES.** ❖
The problem is distribution—getting food to
the people who need it. It is a surprise to learn
that even the hungriest of countries export food.
Ethiopia, Somalia, India, and the United States,
grow food and sell it overseas for animal feed.

Forty percent of this corn will feed livestock rather than humans.

The World Bank estimates that over forty percent of the world's grain and sixty percent of processed fish are fed, not to people, but to livestock. If all that grain were grown to feed people, everyone on earth could eat regularly.

Each year the United Nations publishes research which shows that enough food is grown to feed everyone in the entire world.

People are hungry because of the politics and economics of food distribution. Brazil is the second largest exporter of food in the world. Bananas, corn, fruit, and beans once grew abundantly there. But now more than twenty-five percent of the land is owned by large companies which grow soy beans for export. In the United States corn and soy beans are grown to fatten cattle, chickens, and pigs. Peru has the largest anchovy fishmeal industry in the world. This

protein-rich fish flour is sold to Europe and the
U.S. to feed dogs, cats and chickens.

❖ AREN'T THERE JUST TOO ❖ MANY PEOPLE TO FEED?

Feeding the hungry does not increase over-
population but decreases it. Whenever hunger
decreases, population growth goes down. When
the quality of life is improved, people want to
have fewer children.

Poor people in agricultural areas need large
families. Children help with the farm work and
are the only "social security" for aged parents.
The higher the death rate of children, the more
children agricultural people need to have.

In Kerala, India, when pregnant women were
cared for and given food, more babies survived.
Soon, women decided to have fewer children.
The population growth rate declined to below
two percent. Kerala, India, is one example of
many described in the World Development
Report showing how decreasing hunger actually
helps to decrease infant mortality. Women can
then have fewer children.

❖ ARE POOR PEOPLE HUNGRY ❖ BECAUSE THEY ARE LAZY?

No. They don't have the power, energy, or
opportunity to make life better. The poorer
people are, the less they are paid for their work.

Migrant workers in the United States are paid a dollar an hour, sometimes less.

Forty percent of the world's people earn only fifteen percent of the world's income. Poor people do not have political or economic power. In El Salvador teenagers harvest the coffee crop. They work all day to fill a twenty-five-pound basket and are paid sixty-five cents a day.

As one account of a landless laborer in Bangladesh reminds us, being unemployed does not mean being lazy. In the laborers own words, "Today I went to three villages looking for work. I found nothing. No work means no rice. Yesterday I couldn't find work, and I ate nothing all day . . . Each day I ask myself, how will I live? How will my children live?"

❖ WHY DON'T THE HUNGRY ❖ GROW WHAT THEY NEED?

In most countries where hunger exists, five percent of the people—the upper class—own seventy-five percent of the land. Ownership and control of land by small farmers is essential for a decrease in world hunger.

International companies have purchased agricultural land from small farmers, sometimes by force. Some governments have simply taken land from farmers. A priest who was thrown out of Guatemala describes what happened to local

Most countries spend more on the military than on feeding the hungry.

farmers. "One by one they are simply put in jail until they sign over the land they own."

Think about this Filipino farmer who tells about his experience. "After the war, we became tenants . . . our crops were corn and fiber . . . when the banana company started here, we did not know what to do . . . we were just told to leave. Three weeks later they bulldozed our crops and the posts of our houses. So what could we do?"

When people cannot grow food, they must

buy it. In the U.S. food is cheap compared to other countries. In Mexico, thirty-two percent of an average income is spent on food. In China, fifty percent of a family's income is spent on food.

❖ WHAT ELSE AFFECTS WORLD ❖ FOOD SUPPLIES?

War destroys homes, grocery stores, and crops—all access to food. War uproots people. Refugees have no way to grow or buy food. The biggest increase in starving people has been caused by war, not hurricanes or earthquakes.

War is expensive. Most countries, rich or poor, spend huge amounts of money on the military. Tanks are built instead of irrigation ditches. People are paid to be soldiers instead of farmers. Every day the governments of the world spend millions of dollars on the military. The money spent in one day on war could feed the world's hungry children for a year.

What can you do? What can one person do that can make a difference?

Remember Eloy Casorla, the sixteen-year-old who left home after his father was killed? First he became just another street kid. Most street kids, in South America or the United States, survive less than a year. But Eloy was a survivor. He didn't get shot or starve. Eloy became a successful carpenter because someone cared.

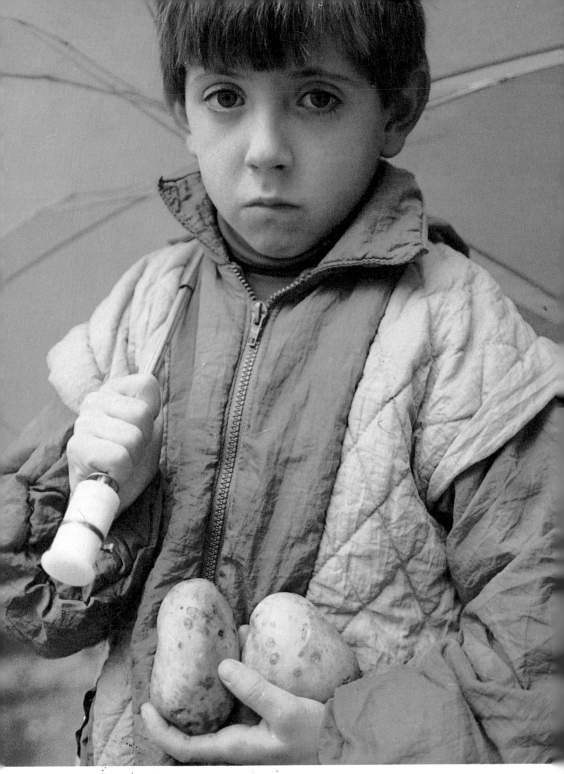

Refugees constitute the largest growing number of starving people.

One night Eloy had stayed in a street shelter run by the Daughters of Charity. A few of these women had converted a chicken coop into a carpentry shop. Their goals were simple—get the kids off the streets, feed them, and then teach them a marketable skill. Eloy learned woodworking. These women now direct seven shelters that work with over a thousand homeless youth.

These next chapters describe what people are doing to help put an end to world hunger. Some efforts take only a few minutes. Some take a lifetime.

❖ QUESTIONS TO ASK YOURSELF ❖

Hunger has been called the world's silent catastrophe. You are taking the first step toward seeking a solution by learning about the problem. Let's take a look at some of the issues surrounding hunger. 1) Who does hunger affect? 2) What is chronic hunger and how does it affect the body? 3) If there is enough food for everyone, why are people starving? 4) What do you think the biggest cause of starvation is and why?

chapter

3

A MILLION CANDLES BURNING

SEPTEMBER 1990—A MILLION CANDLES burned around the world, flickering with one hope, one prayer, one dream: that children could grow up with full bellies and strong minds, free from hunger.

These candles celebrated the first time in history that leaders from 156 countries gathered to talk about children. This meeting was the World Summit for Children. The result was a document: World Declaration on the Survival, Development, and Protection of Children.

World Summit for Children talked about one problem: death from hunger. The declaration pledged that by the year 2000, nine out of ten children would live past their fifth birthday.

Japan was not going to send a delegate to the World Summit. Three teenagers wrote a petition, collected over 16,000 signatures, and then spoke with Mr. Toshiki Kaifu, Japan's prime minister. Their petition read: "Ending hunger is

These children wait for clean drinking water, something most people take for granted.

One goal of the World Summit is to reduce the number of women who die during pregnancy and birth by half.

important for all children as well as for Japan. We believe it is important that *all* leaders attend this World Summit." Mr. Kaifu attended the World Summit for Children.

These three teenagers made a difference. You can make a difference. Learn the facts, talk to others, and then take action.

After the World Summit for Children the United Nations delegation also wrote a document that for the first time in history listed the rights of all children. This document is the **United Nations Convention of the Rights of the Child**. All leaders agreed to begin the political action needed to make these rights legally binding in their own countries.

Here's the list of your rights as a child of this world:

- to be loved and receive affection
- to have enough food to grow and to be free from chronic hunger
- to have enough medical care so sickness is not part of being alive
- to attend school, freely
- to play
- to have a home, a name, a nationality
- to receive special help if handicapped
- to receive priority assistance during disasters
- to learn an occupation—become an independent individual

All children have the right to food and basic health.

- grow up in the spirit of peace and harmony
- have these same rights regardless of race, color, sex, religion, nationality, or social origin

What good are rights if children can't survive? The World Summit identified that the first step was providing food and basic health care for pregnant women and to children.

The World Summit made these plans to increase child survival.

1. Reduce the death rate of children under five. The Child Survival Campaign was begun, and is working. Death rates are decreasing because of organizations like CARE and UNICEF.

2. Reduce the numbers of women who die during pregnancy and childbirth by half. In 1990 every minute of every day a woman died in pregnancy or birthing.

3. Clean up the drinking water—develop simple water systems so that all children drink disease-free and pollution-free water.

4. Educate all children. In developing countries, the children least likely to go to school are girls. When mothers know how to read, they improve their life skills. Their babies are twice as likely to stay alive.

The dream to end world hunger that first came alive with a million candles, has become a plan. The work to make this plan go into effect now depends on individuals. At the end of this book is a list of organizations, what they do, and their addresses. When one person acts, one part of the world changes. As a citizen of the world, light your own candle.

❖ QUESTIONS TO ASK YOURSELF ❖

The only way to permanently end world hunger is for the world's governments to get involved. This process has begun to a certain extent. 1) What was the result of the 1990 World Summit for Children? 2) What rights do all children have according to the Untied Nations?

People like the late Audrey Hepburn are working with UNICEF
to help children all over the world.

chapter

4

HOW YOU CAN HELP

WHAT CAN YOU DO ABOUT WORLD HUNGER?
There are four main ways to help: providing
service, giving money, using your purchasing
power, and influencing others. The first step is
learning.

❖ LEARN ❖

Read the newspaper. Watch the news on TV.
As you begin to take notice of articles—perhaps
an update on Somalia, Haiti or the refugees in
Europe—you begin to realize that hunger is a
problem everywhere.

Sassy magazine has featured an article about
teenage migrant farm workers. These teenagers
work in Ohio or Michigan, or wherever crops
need picking. The living and working conditions
of Imelda and Jesabel were described—over-
crowded trailers, and work from five a.m. until
dark for a dollar an hour. Imelda began picking
strawberries when she was seven. Sometimes

their families do not have enough to eat, so the girls keep picking. They do not attend school.

Suggestion for action:
- Tell a friend what you have learned. Not many people know that forty thousand people die every day from hunger.
- Suggest a hunger project at your school or service club or religious group.
- Stick your neck out. The Giraffe Project is an organization that encourages kids and adults to "stick their necks out for the common good." This project will send you kits with ideas for activities kids can do. Write to: Giraffe Project, Education Dept., PO Box 759, Langley, WA 98260. Phone: (206) 321-0757

Learn more about how to influence people by joining the world anti-hunger lobby group, RESULTS. Write to them at: 236 Massachusetts Ave. NE, Washington, DC 20002-4980. Phone: 202 543 9340. Ask them to send the free brochure about how lobbying works.

RESULTS has local groups in every state. They work to create political action to fight hunger and poverty in their communities. RESULTS will tell you the name and phone number of the local group near you. Attend a meeting or ask for their newsletter.

Migrant workers often work and live under inhumane conditions.

Former US President Jimmy Carter volunteered for Habitat for Humanity.

Write to Bread for the World, a Christian Citizen's Movement fighting world hunger, at: 802 Rhode Island Avenue, N.E. Washington, DC 20018. Phone: 202 269 0200. Ask for their media packet. This packet includes news updates, the names and addresses of political leaders who are taking action, guidelines for writing and submitting letters to the editors of newspapers, bytes for media messages, fact sheets, sample letters, and encouragement. They publish pamphlets and books that describe current anti-hunger projects.

Read *Kids Ending Hunger* by Apple and Sage
Howard. *Monsoon* by John Ballard is the first
teen novel written about ending world hunger.
This story tells how one teenager risks all to
do something about the starvation in India.
Frances Temple's *Grab Hands and Run* is a
story about an El Salvadoran family fleeing to
Canada.

Once you learn, you can influence other
people. Tell a friend, your parents, or teachers.
Talk to groups of kids, like the Key Club,
the Rotary, or the Green Club. Share what you
are thinking. Get excited. Get talking.

❖ TALK ❖

When you have a speech assignment, speak
about world hunger. Stories from *Kids Ending
Hunger* offer exciting material. For your next
assigned research project, write about world
hunger. Tell one person. Then there will be two
of you who care . . . then four . . . then the whole
world. Change starts with you.

❖ WRITE ❖

For more facts, write Food First, 398 60th
Street, Oakland, CA 94618. Phone: 510 654
4400. Ask for their free pamphlet "Hunger
Myths & Facts" (twenty copies for $5) or their
video, *The Business of Hunger* ($30 rental). Food
First is the oldest "think tank" studying world

President Clinton
The White House
1600 Pennsylvania Ave. NW
Washington, DC 20500

Date

Dear Mr. President:
I am writing about world hunger. This is important
to me because 40,000 kids are dying every day. I
have been reading a book about world hunger. I
think you should know that _____
_____

One thing I am asking you to do is support the
work of Representative Tony Hall, Chairman of the
Congressional Hunger Caucus. Thank you for reading my letter and thank you for thinking about
world hunger.

Sincerely,

Your name

hunger. Their comic book, "Food First Comic," is the first comic book about hunger.

Write to your state representative and federal congressperson. Simply say that you think decreasing hunger is important. Send a copy to your local newspaper or to the President. Let people know that you care.

Letters make a difference. The goals written at the first World Summit for Children in 1990 were taken back to each country to be signed and acted upon. President Bush was one of the few who didn't sign.

The following spring, people from RESULTS and people like you sent letters to President Bush. They pointed out that over 135 other countries had signed the agreement. Iran, Iraq, Libya, South Africa, and the United States had not. The president signed.

Here's an easy outline for your letter. One page is plenty. For more ideas, read *The Kid's Guide to Social Action*.

If you write to a senator or representative, use the same form. Your librarian can help you find the names of your congressional representatives.

Senator:
The Honorable————
U.S. Senate
Washington, DC
    20501

Representative:
The Honorable————
U.S. House of
Representatives
Washington, DC
    20501

World Leader:
(Name of the person)
(Name of the country) Embassy
United Nations
United Nations Plaza
New York, New York 10017

Remember:
1. Include your full name and address so you can receive a reply.
2. State your concern all in the first line.
3. Keep to one concern per letter. A brief letter is a strong letter.
4. Be polite and to the point. State a few facts about world hunger.
5. Write neatly and mail it promptly.

You can call, too. In the United States, federal government switchboard operators connect you to specific departments. Call 202 245 6999. If you want to speak to a member of Congress, call 202 224 3121. If you want to go to the top, leave a message for the President at his White House number, 202 456 1414.

❖ **QUESTIONS TO ASK YOURSELF** ❖

There are many ways to become active in the fight against world hunger. Let's think about some of them. 1) How can you learn more about world hunger? 2) If you were to write to a government official, to whom would you write and what would you say?

chapter

5

MORE CHOICES: WORKING AGAINST HUNGER

JOIN AN ORGANIZATION. HELP WITH LOCAL community projects, or help hungry people around the world.

In Omaha, Nebraska, thirteen-year-old Jeff Williamson and his friends joined an effort by Habitat for Humanity, an organization that builds and renovates homes for the homeless. You can help too. Write to: Habitat for Humanity, 121 Habitat St., Americus, GA 31709-3498. Phone: 912 924 6935.

Join an international group and light your candle with them. Some of these are: Save the Children, Seva, UNICEF, World Hunger Year, World Vision, CARE, Project Concern, American Jewish World Service, and Maryknoll.

Addresses and descriptions of each organization are in the appendix.

Here are some actions you can take:

Adopt a goat. The organization INSA sends a

Some families help support themselves by doing menial work such as building cardboard boxes.

pregnant goat to a Haitian family. One goat can provide milk, cheese, and baby goats. For information, write to INSA, International Service Association for Health, PO Box 15086, Atlanta, GA 30333. You can also ask for their video showing how puppets made by volunteers are used to teach health and nutrition.

You or your family could also have a dairy cow sent to a village that will use the cow for milk. The Heifer Project International sends farm animals to rural villages and farmers. Or encourage a club to have a fund-raiser and then choose: send a duck ($1), a whole flock of ducks or chickens ($10), a swarm of bees ($25), or a goat ($150).

Save the Children, CARE, and UNICEF are working to make the Child Survival Campaign successful. More than a million lives have been saved. Help one child, through CARE, for less than forty cents a day. Write to Deborah Scotti, CARE Membership Director, 151 Ellis Street, Atlanta, GA 30303.

You can "Clown Around for Kids." Save the Children will supply information and red clown noses for fundraisers. Just write and ask for a campaign booklet and lots of noses: Save the Children, 54 Wilton Road, Westport, CT 06880.

Have your school adopt a sister city. For details write to Sister Cities International, 120 S. Payne St., Alexandria, VA 22314. Phone: 703 836 3535.

Teach children about how chronic hunger can cause blindness. Collect pennies and send them to Helen Keller International and International Eye Foundation. See page 61.

Many organizations have campaign kits with free posters, pamphlets and videos. For example, Trick-or-treat for UNICEF on Halloween.

Oxfam was founded in 1942 to help those starving in Europe as a result of World War II. Whoopi Goldberg wrote the introduction to *South and North, East and West,* stories told by children from all around the world. Proceeds go to Oxfam's projects.

Join Oxfam's *Fast for a World Harvest.*

Living in poverty can result in the starvation of body and mind.

Make a friendship box. For information, write to the American Red Cross, National Headquarters, International/Youth Services, Attn: Friendship Boxes, Washington, DC 20006.

Help a local program. Groups usually active in communities are the United Way, Salvation Army, Department of Social Services, Rotary, and Kiwanis. You can call the Chamber of Commerce or your library and ask, "What local groups have programs to help the hungry?"

A mother in Berkeley, California, saw an old man rummaging for food in a garbage can. She started a food re-gathering program so leftover

but good food from restaurants and stores would be given to the hungry and homeless. Many young people worked with her. For information, write to Carolyn North, Daily Bread, 2447 Prince St., Berkeley, CA 94705.

Another program, Berkeley Cares, uses a voucher system so that donations are translated into vouchers or tickets for hungry people to obtain their basic needs—food, shelter, laundry, medical, and transportation to schools and job training.

Choose a personal action. Buy a jar of peanut butter for a food basket. Suggest a food basket program at your school or church.

Eat low on the food chain. Take action everyday by keeping one meal meatless. Here's how eating low helps.

A hamburger means a dead cow somewhere. Producing four hamburgers requires: sixteen pounds of grain and soybeans, at least 2500 gallons of water, and the energy from one gallon of gasoline. Write to AFSC, 1501 Cherry St., Philadelphia, PA 19102. They will send a slide show about the role of the hamburger in the world. Read *Diet for a Small Planet*.

Over fifty more ways for individuals to help end hunger are listed in *Kids Ending Hunger, What Can We Do ?* Here are a few favorites.

Buy UNICEF cards instead of commercial ones. Your money helps hungry children.

UNICEF and the Red Cross are the only two organizations awarded the Nobel Peace Prize. Help them and you help the world.

IDEX—this agency will match your school with another school that needs supplies:

End Hunger Network—write and you will receive a list of rock stars and movie stars who are concerned about world hunger. Invite a star to sing at your school's anti-hunger concert. Write to your favorite actors, or authors. Tell them about world hunger—ask them to help too. Bob Geldof once got us singing about it . . . *we are the world.*

Audrey Hepburn worked in the refugee camps of Somalia, told the world about it, and got people caring.

Remember *Where the Wild Things Are*, by Maurice Sendack? In *The Big Book for Peace*, Sendack draws for the hungry, asking us to imagine a world where there are no hunger monsters and all children have enough to eat.

On April 19, 1993 in Atlanta, Georgia, former President Carter greeted 10,000 volunteers who were about to give free vaccinations along with a ticket to a Michael Jackson concert.

In 1993 the work of Jimmy Carter was saluted by CARE International.

Cesar Chavez was a model for nonviolent action and courage. He fought the injustices that kept migrant workers in poverty.

At the 1993 Academy Awards, Elizabeth Taylor was given the Gene Hershell Humanitarian Award for Service. She had spoken out about AIDS.

It's your choice. Choose to act. An action can be as simple as telling someone about world hunger or as long-term as becoming a volunteer. Sometimes a phone call begins a journey that becomes a lifetime job. Individual actions make the difference.

Which candle will you light?
Learn, then talk, phone, write, act.

❖ QUESTIONS TO ASK YOURSELF ❖

There are many ways to help fight world hunger. The following questions might help you narrow down the choices. 1) What kind of world-hunger project or volunteer job interests you? 2) What events can you and your friends or your class organize to raise money for the hungry? 3) What world-hunger organizations are available in your community?

chapter

6

MAKE A DIFFERENCE

JUSTIN SIGNED UP FOR A WORLD HUNGER Seminar. He had no idea what he was getting into. His advisor said, "Try it. You'll be surprised." He was.

At the start of the first class, the instructor, Dave Harmon, held up a small book, *World Hunger, Twelve Myths*, and began explaining how the course started three years ago.

"I was teaching ethics and the class was arguing about the moral complexities of world hunger. Several students were struck by the grim fact that millions of people die from hunger."

"Let's do something," one student said.

"But what?" The others challenged.

"What could I say?" Dave looked at the class. No one said a word. The ethics class had learned one basic rule: learn, think, and then act. The class decided to study world hunger and then they formed an action group, WAAS: World Awareness and Action Society. They de-

Despite the devastation of hunger and poverty, there is hope among
the children of the world.

fined their purpose: to increase awareness of world hunger at a personal level. That meant personal action. One student decided to design this course.

The WAAS group joined RESULTS, a national organization, from whom they obtained information about political action. Then they wrote personal letters to congress people.

To increase awareness of hunger, the class created ads for the radio and newspaper for World Food Day on October 17th. They organized a banquet. People came to the cafeteria and sat down to eat. Some were given a plateful of steak and potatoes. Most were given a bowl or rice—or nothing. The reality and injustice of hunger amidst plenty suddenly became real.

Forty thousand people a day dying. What else could they do?

They found out that one place for action was Nicaragua, Central America, where the infant mortality rate was about twenty percent.

The WAAS group decided to join the Friendship City Exchange program, in which a city in the United States is paired with a city overseas that wants assistance.

Teotecacinte, Nicaragua, had voted to participate as a sister city. The city council asked for help in building a new water system. Eight students from WAAS joined eight students from Boulder, Colorado and traveled to Teotecacinte with tools and supplies.

The new water system brought clean water to Teotecacinte. In 1992 the death rate for children dropped from twenty percent to less than five percent.

The following year another group of college students went to Teotecacinte to help rebuild the grade school which had been shelled during the war.

Dave Harmon commented, "I remembered watching children walking to that school, each one carrying a chair. Inside the school there was no furniture, nothing. I turned to the college students—'shall we go?'—The whole class signed up. And then other people from the college volunteered to go with us.

"They and the people from Teotecacinte rebuilt the school. The people started a carpentry shop and a sewing co-operative.

"Every year now a group of students and community volunteers brings supplies and people-power for a two-week trip to Teotecacinte. The people there are asking for help with two new projects—building a health clinic and starting a women's high-school scholarship fund."

❖ QUESTIONS TO ASK YOURSELF ❖

It doesn't take much effort to get involved in a project you believe in. 1) What class project can you think of to help raise awareness about world hunger? 2) Is there a Friendship City Exchange in your area?

chapter

7

"IF PEOPLE WEREN'T EATING, WHAT ELSE MATTERED?" FRANCES MOORE LAPPÉ

Why is there hunger? Twenty years ago Frances Lappe discovered that the people who control the land and the flow of money are the ones who regulate the availability of food. In some countries the government has this control. In others it's the international mega-companies or the military.

In 1971, Frances Moore Lappe wrote *Diet for a Small Planet.* Twenty years ago this was a revolutionary book. It is now sold world-wide.

In 1975, Ms. Lappé and Joseph Collins founded the Institute for Food and Development Policy. Its mission is to improve the lives of the hungry and oppressed. The Institute publishes books, comic books, and videos.

In Guatemala in 1992, Rigoberta Menchú received the Nobel Peace Prize. She spoke out for the basic human rights of the indigenous people in her country and all countries.

In the United States, Cesar Chavez was an undaunted fighter for the rights of migrant workers. He was assassinated in 1993.

In Denver, Colorado, Jossy Eyre used $500 of her own funds to start the Women's Bean Project. Homeless women became self-sufficient while working together to package an Anasazi Ten-Bean Soup that is now sold throughout the state (call 303 292-1919 to order).

In Miami, Florida, thirteen-year-old Alison Stieglitz began a project to feed the hungry on Thanksgiving. The first year she passed out fifteen baskets of food to elderly people who were home-bound. Today, Hungry and Homeless serves breakfast and bag lunches each Sunday to over two hundred fifty people.

❖ COMMUNITY GROUPS ❖

In Glenwood Springs, Colorado, police officers started a program so every homeless child would have presents and dinner on Christmas.

Six Maryknoll sisters were in Panama when the U.S. invaded in 1989. They set up a rehabilitation community and worked with the three thousand people whose homes were destroyed. Together, they housed, fed, and found jobs for everyone.

At fifteen, Lucia Lopez joined a parish youth group to work with the hungry and homeless. Now she speaks out internationally about the

By forming the action group World Awareness and Action Society, (WAAS), the students in Dave Harmon's ethics class were able to help these children in Teotecacinte, Nicaragua.

communities of women who have established over seven thousand food kitchens in Lima, Peru.

❖ INTERNATIONAL AGENCIES ❖

These organizations give food, medicine, or supplies during emergencies: CARE, Catholic Relief, American Jewish World Service, and UNICEF.

Some organizations teach people job skills or new ways to grow food. They include the Church World Service, Oxfam, Partners of the

Americas, Project Concern, and the United Nations Development Programme.

Other organizations, such as Africare and the Heifer Project International, provide tools, seeds, farm animals, and equipment like tractors, saws, lumber, and books for schools.

Some organizations speak out, providing information, increased awareness and encouraging action. They include RESULTS, Bread for the World, Institute for Food and Development Policy, Children's Defense Fund, IDEX, The Hunger Project, and the End Hunger Network.

One by one, we each make a difference.

❖ QUESTIONS TO ASK YOURSELF ❖

Take a step toward fighting world hunger by learning the effects of other people's actions.
1) How are local efforts making a difference?
2) How do international agencies help?

chapter

8

WHAT HAVE WE DONE? WHERE ARE WE GOING?

THE BIGGEST PROBLEMS IN OUR WORLD ARE hunger and poverty. Chronic hunger exists because of man-made causes. Countries have the resources and money to end world hunger, but it will not decrease unless ending hunger becomes a priority.

One single action by Congress can help the work of all the international agencies. Silence is understood as indifference or consent. Speak up—by phone or letter.

In the 1960s U.S. President John F. Kennedy set two goals for the United States: one was putting a person on the moon, and the other was eliminating world hunger. Every one was very excited about people walking on the moon. How many even realized that world hunger existed?

"If there is the political will ... it should be possible to overcome the worst aspects of wide-

*spread hunger and malnutrition within one
generation."*

National Academy of Sciences

Have we had the political will to change
things since *Diet for a Small Planet* was published
twenty-five years ago? Have we decreased starvation since the Childrens' Survival Campaign
began working toward the goals of the 1990
World Summit for Children?

We have made a few steps. People are beginning to realize what has to be done.

The total number of chronically hungry
people in the world has increased. But some
programs are beginning to work. Fewer children
are dying from hunger-related causes. Tentative
new figures from UNICEF suggest that 35,000
—a drop from 40,000—die each day. According
to CARE, the number of infant deaths per
1,000 births has dropped worldwide since 1975.

We still have a long way to go.

Wars continue to destroy farm land and
homes. More people than ever are refugees.
Most of the foreign aid is spent on guns and
bullets instead of books, tools, and seeds. International companies buy up the best land, cut
down the rain forests, and destroy people's
ability to feed themselves. Prejudice closes the
school doors. Oppressive actions keep people
poor by paying less than liveable wages.

Some oppressed people are speaking out.

The indigenous people of Brazil, the Guarani, speak through their chief, Cacique Altino:

"We do not destroy nature. We do not kill an animal unless we need it. Many of our problems would disappear if we had a place where we knew we could grow our food and no one would come and say it is theirs and take it."

Women are beginning to speak out—Rigoberta Menchu in Guatemala, Wangari Maathai in Africa, Mary Robinson in Ireland.

Women grow most of the world's food, feed the children, and teach them.

Margaret Mead, well-known anthropologist, once said, "Never doubt that a group of concerned citizens can change the world. It is the only thing that ever has."

❖ QUESTIONS TO ASK YOURSELF ❖

Sometimes the battle against world hunger seems overwhelming. It often helps to start by looking at what has been accomplished, and then tackling one thing that needs to be done. These questions can help you sort that out. 1) What general steps have we made toward eliminating world hunger? 2) Can you imagine a world without hunger? 3) What single step can you take to work toward that goal?

GLOSSARY

chronic hunger Never having enough to eat.

dehydration A condition in which body tissues are deprived of water.

famine Extreme scarcity of food—hunger, starvation.

immunize (verb) To help the body resist disease.

immunization (noun) Weakened germs given to make the body produce antibodies against the germs to create a defense mechanism.

lobby (verb) To talk to legislators in order to influence government proceedings. Example: "They are lobbying for peace."

lobby (noun) Those people, collectively, who seek to talk to legislators. Example: "The peace lobby is here to see the senator."

malnutrition The lack of sufficient food to provide the body with what it needs to sustain health.

polio A viral inflammation of the nerves, sometimes resulting in muscular problems.

voucher A piece of paper that represents the truth of something.

ORGANIZATIONS TO CONTACT

Africare
440 R St. NW Washington DC 20001

American Jewish World Service
1290 Avenue of the Americas New York, NY 10104

Bread for the World
802 Rhode Island Ave. NE Washington DC 20018

CARE
660 First Ave. New York, NY 10016

Catholic Relief Services
209 W. Fayette St. Baltimore, MD 21201

Church World Services
475 Riverside Drives New York, NY 10115

End Hunger Network
222 N. Beverly Drive, Beverly Hills, CA 90210

Heifer Project International
PO Box 808 Little Rock, AR 72203

The Hunger Project
1 Madison Avenue New York, NY 10010

Helen Keller International
15 W. 16th St. New York, NY 10011

International Eye Foundation
7801 Norfolk Bethesda, MD 20814

IDEX
827 Valencia Street, San Francisco, CA 94110

OXFAM
115 Broadway, Boston, MA 02116

Project Concern
3550 Afton Road, San Dieo, CA 92123

RESULTS
236 Massachusetts Ave. NE Suite 300 Washington
  DC 20002 4980

Save the Children
54 Wilton Road, Westport, CT 06880

UNICEF
333 E. 38th St. New York, NY 10016

**World Day for Overcoming Extreme Poverty—
Fourth World Movement**
7600 Willow Hill Drive, Landover, MD 20785
  phone: 301 336 9489

Young America Cares/United Way of America
701 N. Fairfax St Alexandria, VA 22314
  phone: 703 836 7100 ext 445

Further Reading

❖ NONFICTION ❖

Howard, Tracy Apple. *Kids Ending Hunger, What Can We Do?* Kansas City: Andrews and McMeel, 1992.

Hunger 1992, Second Annual Report on the State of World Hunger. Washington, DC: Bread for the World Institute on Hunger & Development, 1992.

Lappé, Frances Moore. *Diet for a Small Planet.* New York: Ballantine Books, 1971.

—— and Collins, Joseph. *World Hunger—Twelve—Myths.* San Francisco: The Institute for Food and Development Policy, 1986.

Lewis, Barbara A. *The Kid's Guide to Social Action.* Minneapolis: Free Spirit Publishing, 1991.

Williams, Sonja. *Exploding the Hunger Myths.* San Francisco: The Institute for Food and Development Policy, 1987.

❖ FICTION ❖

Temple, Fances, *Grab Hands and Run.* New York: Orchard Books, Watts, 1993

——. *Taste of Salt: A Story of Modern Haiti.* New York: Orchard Books, Watts, 1992.

INDEX

B

blindness
   Helen Keller International, 43, 17
   International Eye Foundation, 17, 43
Bolivia, 12
Brazil
   land owned by large companies, 19
   merchants' death squads, 7
   not enough to eat, 11
   Rio de Janeiro, 7
   second largest food exporter, 19
   homeless children, 7

C

CARE, 31, 41, 43, 46, 53, 57
children
   as social security, 20
   child survival campaign, 30
   die from starvation, 9
   gunned down, 7
   of migrant farm workers, 33
   saving, Daughters of Charity, 25
   searching for food, 8
   sold, 18
   street, survive less than one year, 23
   too hungry to play, 9
   without homes, 7
clothes
   no-one has extra, 14
coffee
   beans, harvesting at 65¢ a day, 14, 21

D

death, 11, 7, 9, 10
   from fever and diarrhea, 18
   from hunger, 26
   from starvation, 14
   infant death rate, 14, 15
   per 30 of populations, 15
   rates decreasing, through CARE &
      UNICEF, 31

E

Ecuador, 18
electricity
   appliances, lack of, 13

F

food
   adequate, effect on population growth,
      20
   corn & soy beans grown for cattle, 19
   fishmeal, fed to cats & dogs, 20
   gifts of animals, 41, 42
   grain & fish fed to livestock, 19
   is there enough? 18
   lack of, eating roots & dirt, 18
   lack of vitamin A, 17
   malnutrition during pregnancy
   minimum food, defined, 14
   needed after disasters, 10
   percentage income spent on, 23
   searching for ways to find, 8
   vouchers, 45
   women grow most of, 58
   World Food Day, 50
form letters
   to President Clinton, 38
   to senators, 39
   to representatives, 39

H

homelessness, 7, 11
   homes for homeless, 41
   rehabilitation community, Panama, 53
hunger
   affects the world, 11
   among US migrant farm workers, 34
   causes blindness, 17
   chronic hunger, defined, 14
   daily, 40,000 children die from, 9
   damages the brain, 17
   due to war, 23
   effects of decreasing, 20
   eliminating, 56
   exists from man-made causes, 56
   harms the human spirit, 17
   increases damage from other diseases,
      17
   injustice amidst plenty, 50
   is a problem everywhere, 33
   kills slowly, 16
   millions die from, 48
   rock stars, concerned, 46
   too hungry to play, 9
   two out of ten hurt by, 14
   why is there, 18, 52
hustling
   shining shoes, stealing, washing cars, 12

I

India
   Kerala, study, 20

L
land ownership, 19, 21
  by coercion, 22
  by international companies, 21
  by small farmers, 21
  by upper classes, 21
  that destroys peoples' ability to feed
    themselves, 57

N
Nicaragua
  clean water project, 50
  grade school rebuilt, 51

O
orphanage, 10
Oxfam, 43, 55

P
Peace Corps, 18
Peru
  anchovy fishmeal industry, 19
    sold to feed cats & dogs, 20
  food kitchens in Lima, 53
Phillipines, the, 22
poverty
  earning less than $600 per annum, 15
  in poorer countries, 9
  poor people are paid less, 20, 21

R
reading
  never learning, 15
Red Cross, 10, 44, 46

S
school
  basic human right, 52

could go, but lacking clothes, pencils,
  etc., 14
educate all children, 31
impossible or meaningless, 11
never attending, 16
social awareness
  in Sassy magazine, 33

T
telephone numbers, organizations, 34, 36,
  37, 40, 41, 53

U
United Nations
  child survival campaign, 43
  Convention of the Rights of the Child,
    29
  development program, 55
  food production research, 19
  UNICEF, 31, 41, 46, 55, 57
  World Development Report, 20
  World Summit for Children, 26, 39

W
war, 23
  costs of military, 23
  destruction, 57
water
  clean, 31
  clean up, 31
  for cattle, 45
  new system, Teotecacinte, 50
  no running, 13
  polluted, 16
work, 21
World Bank, 19

ABOUT THE AUTHOR

For the past decade, psychologist Nancy Bohac Flood's work has been focused on children—evaluating, counseling and teaching. She has written extensively and is the creator of a therapeutic board game.

Dr. Flood conducts conferences and workshops about abuse and neglect, learning disabilities, play therapy, and evaluation of treatment issues. She now teaches at Colorado Mountain College, and is a freelance writer.

PHOTO CREDITS: The Helen Keller Institute, (p. 16), UNICEF (pp. 42, 44, 49), Dave
  Harmon (p. 54), AP/Wide World Photos (all other photos)
PHOTO RESEARCH: Vera Ahmadzadeh
DESIGN: Kim Sonsky